path
to
peace

Shi Wuling

Venerable Wuling is an American Buddhist nun
of the Pure Land tradition of Mahayana Buddhism.

Amitabha Publications, Chicago, 60532
© 2006 by Amitabha Publications
Some rights reserved. No part of this book may not be altered without permission
from the publisher. Reprinting is allowed for non-profit use.

12 11 10 09   5 6 7 8 9
ISBN: 978-1-59975-354-6
Library of Congress Control Number:2005938180

Reprinted by:
Amitabha Buddhist Retreat Centre
PO Box 216, Nanango Qld 4615
Tel: 07-4171-0421 Fax: 7-4171-0413
www.abrc.org.au

In Appreciation

With love and gratitude,

I thank my parents

Milton and Evelyn Bolender.

nurture love,

give joy,

be compassionate,

create peace.

january 1

before we can help,
we need to understand.

before we can understand,
we need to listen.

before we can listen,
we need to be quiet.

january 2

one does not

arrive at happiness,

one travels its path.

january 3

world peace will begin

when we end the wars

within each of us.

january 4

we can influence others

for the good

by the good

that we are thinking.

january 5

compassion

ushers sadness out

guides happiness in.

january 6

why seek outside?

everything we need

is already

within us.

january 7

in developing compassion, we care for

those we love

those we know.

eventually we will even care for

those we do not like

those we do not know.

january 8

peace within

creates beauty without.

january 9

may all beings
become messengers of peace
in times of chaos and conflict.

may they
become the calm voice of reason
in times of anguish and anger.

january 10

gentleness is the companion of joy
tenderness of compassion
serenity of wisdom.

january 11

happiness lies in the smile,

not in the object

that inspired the smile.

january 12

to listen

and to be listened to

is the way to

understanding and peace.

january 13

understand things as they really are.

do not mistake
the reflection of the moon in the water
for the moon.

january 14

the generous person gives

not just what they have

but of who they are.

january 15

when we are

kind and generous to others,

we will receive

thoughtfulness and love.

january 16

contentment

is not the fulfillment of what we want

rather the appreciation of what we have.

january 17

just as dew refreshes

the wilting flower,

tenderness restores

the grieving heart.

january 18

better

than trying to control others

is trying to control oneself.

january 19

yesterday is a memory ~

~ tomorrow but a dream

our reality
is the present moment.

january 20

transform

anger with patience,

doubt with understanding,

selfishness with generosity.

january 21

sincerity in words
      engenders trust.
sincerity in thought
      engenders pure living.
sincerity in generosity
      engenders loving-kindness.

january 22

may ignorance give way to understanding.
may hatred yield to compassion.
may war surrender to peace.

january 23

the absence
of expectations
results in
the reduction
of disappointments.

january 24

contentment is born of the capacity

to love impartially

to listen uncritically

to give unconditionally

to forgive unreservedly

to laugh at oneself unaffectedly.

january 25

gently and impartially

comfort the uneasy

give selflessly to those who are in need

teach without reserve those who wish to learn.

january 26

excessive desires lead us to put our
own interests before those of others.
they drain our goodness,
pollute our hearts,
immerse us in animosity.

january 27

dreams fade
bubbles pop
dew evaporates
lightning ceases.

nothing is permanent.

january 28

in the wise and gentle heart

lies the strength

to change the world.

january 29

only when we have compassion

for all beings

will we have true peace.

january 30

smile

be at peace

let go of sadness

forget thoughts of anger

release all regret

realize joy

smile

january 31

the cloud transforms into rain.
   the flower transforms into earth.
      the earth transforms and becomes a flower
                        watered by the rain
                        that was the cloud.

      nothing exists on its own.

                        february 1

with greed comes
animosity, ignorance, pride,
thoughts of self-benefit and discontent.

with generosity comes
loving-kindness, wisdom, humility,
thoughts of all others and great joy.

february 2

austerity can make us hard
and withdrawn...

...indulgence can make us soft
and indifferent.

the middle path
is the balanced way of
compassion,
wisdom,
and insight.

february 3

as we think

so we become.

february 4

awakened ones

    are able to properly help others

because their actions

    are born of wisdom.

february 5

do not resent the heavens for one's fate.
do not blame our problems on others.

realize the negative cause
lies within us,
was created by us,
can only be changed by us,
resolved by us with
understanding,
diligence,
love.

february 6

lying is a hindrance to faith;
laziness, to progress
animosity, to mindfulness
hatred, to deep concentration
and resentment, to wisdom.

february 7

if in our anger, we realize

the other person is suffering,

we can free ourselves

from anger

and from suffering,

which also helps free the other.

february 8

desires that are excessive
preoccupy and distract us.

needs that are reasonable
nurture and sustain us.

february 9

when others hurt us,

we usually react with

anger,

resentment,

and may even wish for retaliation.

but these actions will only prolong our pain,

for to hold resentment in our hearts

only serves to make us feel worse.

february 10

those who give in to desire
are often intoxicated
by sensory indulgence,
not yet realizing
that what pleases today
all too often disappoints tomorrow.

february 11

to truly help others,
do what is
beneficial
correct,
honest.

february 12

reasonable needs are to have
enough food to eat,
adequate clothes to keep warm,
a safe place to live,
good companions
on the path to awakening.

february 13

worry ties us up in knots and
binds us to lifetimes of pain.

who told us to worry?

who said we could not stop?

february 14

anger
the rise of anger
the initial cause of anger
is selfishness.

peace
the rise of peace
the initial cause of peace
is selflessness.

february 15

most of the things

we worry about

never happen.

february 16

listen, carefully
study, diligently
chant, sincerely
think, deeply
love, wisely.

february 17

practicing diligence is like lighting a fire.
if we persist, we will succeed,
if we give up, we will fail.

so often in a new endeavor
there is an initial burst of enthusiasm,
then routine activity…
boredom…
cessation.

with
determination,
the fire will burn strong.

february 18

unkind speech can destroy.

that which is kind
can bring peace
and change the world.

february 19

our thoughts are the precursors
of everything
we do.

what we constantly
tell ourselves
will happen.

february 20

the victor
becomes arrogant,
while the defeated
dwells in pain.

one who is wise,
turns away from both
winning and losing
to live in peace and happiness.

february 21

when we are
forgiving of others
considerate of all beings
contented with what we have
happy in whatever circumstances
we find ourselves

sadness and worry will fade.

february 22

in losing ourselves in

thoughts of ourselves

we lose.

in losing ourselves in

thoughts of others

we truly benefit.

february 23

our animosity and fury

will return to us

    like fine dust

        thrown into the wind,

like flotsam

        cast upstream.

february 24

if we remain open
to the experience of meditation

as we let go
of preconceived ideas and
expectations
we will gradually feel the benefits
as we become more calm
and relaxed.

february 25

peace – the foremost joy.

oneness – the foremost reality.

enlightenment – the foremost freedom.

february 26

heal others' unhappiness with loving-kindness,

their bitterness with compassion.

heal our selfishness with joy at others' success,

our frustration with equanimity.

february 27

in war,

both the winners and losers

lose.

february 28

thoughts give rise to speech;
    speech generates deed;
        deeds become habit;
            and habits form character.
realizing this, one will strive to ensure
that all thoughts
        spring from sincerity and love
        spring forth with compassion.

february 29

                    without thoughts of
this is mine and
that is yours
                    there will be no thoughts of

i do not have.

march 1

have not remorseful thoughts
of *yesterday*
or wishful thoughts
of *tomorrow*.

dwell instead in the present moment.

march 2

the joy of others does not detract
from our own.

rather, it enhances ours
for we are all one.

march 3

everything changes, from
second to second
minute to minute
day to day
lifetime to lifetime.

march 4

we are

not alone

not separate.

we are

one with all beings

one with all existence

one with all the universe.

march 5

in true giving
we will know loving-kindness
    when we wish others
        to be happy.
we will know compassion
    when we wish them
        to be free from suffering.
we will know sympathetic joy
    when we wish their happiness
        to increase.
we will know equanimity
    when we let go of what we desire.

march 6

one who is wise

accepts
what enters his life

and lets go
of what leaves.

march 7

it is right for us to respect and safeguard
        every living creature, for they are one with us.
we are just different aspects of a single being.
we may feel we are dissimilar,
        but in essence we are the same
            with universal beliefs and values.

may the perfection of our true selves
blossom within us as we
        let go of hypocrisy and jealousy,
        bring forth equanimity and wisdom
            to know patience and unity.

march 8

it is time to heal the wounds
born of bitterness and violence,
for if left untended, they will only wreak
irreparable damage.
we reap what we sow.
only sincere thoughts and deeds
will create the joyful world we seek.

may all our hearts and minds bond together
to forge the unshakeable promise
to bring our world everlasting peace.

march 9

cherish and protect this world,
for it is our home
and the home of those
not yet born.
so immense, yet so fragile.
so secure, yet so easily destroyed
by selfishness and hatred.

march 10

it is wise not to judge others,
lest we ourselves
be judged
and found wanting.

march 11

the mind of compassion
knows no bitterness
no judgment
no good   no bad
no right   no wrong
no you   no me.

only the wish for all beings
to be happy.

march 12

in meditation

the goal is to strike a balance between

not indulging the mind as it wanders
and not becoming upset when it does so.

gently but firmly
bring it back to the subject
when it wanders.

march 13

when we learn that
we cannot truly control others,
circumstances,
or things,
we will begin to let go.
we will begin to find freedom.

march 14

when in pain and fear,
remember that all others
suffer as well.

march 15

it is our duty

in everything we do

to do our best with what we have.

no excuses,

no complaints.

march 16

no inferno burns like hatred.

no sea engulfs like desire.

no snare entraps like delusion.

no seizure imprisons like anger.

march 17

with
goodness,
concentration,
and wisdom,
one will understand,
craving will cease
and the other shore will be closer.

march 18

so often, we forget to be thankful.

but while we all have problems,
experience difficult relationships,
fail in our undertakings,
there are many things in our lives
to be thankful for.
all we have to do is
to slow down, take note, value them

and be thankful.

march 19

a blessing is

honest and kind friends

loving and prudent parents

respectful and thoughtful children

wise and compassionate teachers.

march 20

just as the tree whose root

remains intact

will grow again,

anger that is not rooted out

will re-emerge.

march 21

sever delusion

eliminate hatred

touch the clear, bright mind of wisdom within.

awaken.

march 22

suffering arises from
our own untamed minds.

to find genuine happiness,
discipline the mind and
eliminate its negative states.

march 23

unangered among those who argue

unattached among those who cling

unarmed among those who fight

is one who is wise.

march 24

violence only breeds

further violence

never peace.

march 25

why worry about the problem
that cannot be solved?

why worry about that
which can be resolved?

why worry at all?

march 26

as long as a man

    bears resentment in his heart,

        peace will never be his.

march 27

being benevolent and ethical

creating good fortune:

those who are wise

find happiness

here and beyond.

.

march 28

do not strive

to overcome others

but our own shortcomings.

march 29

anger, worry, and bitterness
are not innate in our true nature:
discard them.

compassion, patience, and joy
are the heart of our true nature:
cherish them.

march 30

whether good or bad

our actions will bring results,

good or bad.

march 31

four noble truths:

life is suffering
suffering is caused
suffering can end

the way to its end
is the practice of
morality,
concentration
and wisdom.

april 1

the noble eightfold path

the practice of *wisdom* is accomplished by
right view and right thought;
the practice of *morality* by
right speech , right action,
and right livelihood;
the practice of *concentration* by
right effort, right mindfulness,
and right concentration.

april 2

right view
is understanding
the four noble truths
of
the nature of suffering,
and understanding
the law of causality:

we reap what we sow.

april 3

right thought
is the accordance of our thoughts
with the right view.
it is the letting go of
desires and attachments,
offering happiness to others,
and taking away their bitterness.

april 4

right speech
is the abstention from words
that are false, divisive,
abusive, or frivolous.
it is using words to benefit,
not to harm.

april 5

right action
is the reverence for all life,
and the respect
for the property of others.
it is the practice of
love and non-violence.

april 6

right livelihood
is reflecting
our loving-kindness and
compassion
in the way we earn our living.
it is nurturing and
caring for others
with our work.

april 7

right effort
is enthusiastically approaching
everything we do
in our work, at home,
and in our practice.
it is replacing
unwholesome thoughts
with those that are wholesome.

april 8

right mindfulness
is the state
in which we are aware
of everything that arises in our mind,
but we do so
nonjudgmentally
and without interpretation.

april 9

right concentration
is focusing our attention
on what we choose
without being distracted.
it is the absence of worries,
doubts, and drowsiness.
it is a state of joy and ease.

april 10

do not ask

who has caused me to suffer

but

who i can help

to be free from suffering.

april 11

equanimity is viewing

those we love

and those we hate

and wanting both to be happy.

april 12

each of us has
the *mind of a buddha*
within us,
the *essence of a buddha*
in our true nature.

april 13

listen to others

nonjudgmentally and impartially,

without thoughts of condemnation,

self interest,

evaluation.

april 14

he is able

who thinks

he is able.

april 15

do not be swayed by
external circumstances,
maintain the mind
of quiet joy and serenity within.

april 16

neither fire nor wind,

birth nor death

can erase our good deeds.

april 17

to live a pure, unselfish life,

one must count nothing

as one's own

in the midst of abundance.

april 18

the individual self is not the true self
but a concept
that arises from ignorance.
thoughts and feelings,
which are regarded as real
and, thus, important,
are in reality
illusory and
inconsequential.

april 19

there is no fire like passion,
no shark like hatred,
there is no snare like folly,
no torrent like greed.

april 20

focus on what we are doing
right now.

concentrate.

pay attention.

april 21

may all beings

   savor the nectar of loving-kindness

      to overcome thoughts of controlling others,

bring forth serenity and the insight

      to find happiness and harmony.

april 22

peace is not achieved

through violence,

but through understanding

and compassion.

april 23

with giving,
we can let go of greed.

with patience,
we can dissolve hatred.

with wisdom,
we can sweep away ignorance.

april 24

what we find irksome in another

is a reflection

of what lies within ourselves.

april 25

patience

conquers opposition,

annihilates obstacles,

gives confidence.

april 26

hatred and prejudice
are the enemies of
correct understanding.

april 27

to be happy ourselves,

first we help

somebody else

to be happy.

april 28

anger is like an addiction.

not only did we get upset

the first time,

but we go over and over it,

like watching reruns of a favorite movie.

april 29

to use speech wisely

is to speak truthfully

and in a way

that the listener can accept.

april 30

equanimity is to have

impartial affection for all.

may 1

whatever suffering there is in this world,
it all arises from
desiring only myself to be happy.

whatever joy there is in this world,
it all arises from
desiring to share my happiness with everyone.

may 2

all compound things

are impermanent

and subject to birth and death.

when birth and death no longer exist,

all is silence,

all is joy.

may 3

when looking after ourselves

use compassion;

when looking after others

use compassion.

may 4

neither indulge oneself
nor ignore the one in need
for to do so is self-centered and
heartless.

seek the middle way to
contentment,
humanity,
peace.

may 5

when changes occur
we can choose to adapt
or cling to our ideas.
we can choose to understand
or cling to our pain.

may 6

cultivation is not simply sitting

on a meditation cushion.

cultivation is

correcting our faults,

acting from wisdom and compassion,

having a peaceful and tranquil nature.

may 7

do not be angry with yourself
because of your failure.

do not be envious of others
because of their success.

by not losing oneself
in frustration over what happens
one will live fully every moment.

may 8

in everything you do,

be fully

present in the

m

    o

       m

           e

              n

                 t.

may 9

even a buddha
cannot change that which
we ourselves have destined.

may 10

a drop of rain
falls gently on a leaf and slowly rolls off.
it does not have thoughts of like or dislike.
it does not attach.

likewise,
our minds should see everything clearly,
without differentiation
without attaching.

may 11

the just person is one
who does not arbitrarily
pass judgment,

but thinks deeply and
judges impartially.

may 12

one

who is calm in the face of chaos,
content among the desirous,
peaceful among the violent,

is awakening.

to be happy

let go
of unhappiness.

may 14

we do not achieve things

by way of proclamations and slogans

but through

persistence,

effort, and

enthusiasm.

may 15

there are four things conducive
to the uncovering of wisdom:

association with those who are virtuous

hearing wise and true teachings

listening well and deeply

practicing sincerely.

may 16

one who speaks
    of the teachings
        may be knowledgeable,
but he who incorporates
        the teachings
        into what he does
        is the true practitioner.

may 17

understand

the true nature of form.

understand

the true nature of formlessness.

attach to neither.

may 18

understanding

the reality of impermanence

does away with desire

for material possessions,

for sensual pleasure,

for existence,

and eliminates attachment.

may 19

it is not the other who is our enemy

it is our own lack of understanding.

may 20

the end of the path is
  no birth
  no aging
  no sickness
  no death
it is sublime
  liberation.

may 21

calm the mind ...

let go of pain
let go of sorrow
let go of bitterness.

heal the heart ...

find joy
find serenity
find equanimity.

may 22

the mind
swayed by external conditions
is swept this way and that
by emotions
and loses self-control.

may 23

even the smallest gift,

given from the

unselfish and caring heart,

is a gift of great love.

may 24

one who is liberated

thinks what he wishes

and does not think

any thought he does not wish to.

may 25

the mind of a buddha is
clear and unencumbered
and brings perfect joy.

that of unawakened beings is
clouded and obstructed
and immersed in suffering.

may 26

moral discipline
provides the stability for us to develop
meditative concentration
which enables our
innate wisdom
to arise.

may 27

the awakened person
still showers all with loving-kindness
and understanding
even when
cast out by relatives
scorned by friends
rejected by colleagues
ignored by strangers.

may 28

transform   anger with patience.

transform   evil with good.

transform the miserly with generosity.

transform   the liar with truth.

may 29

subject to

> birth
>
> aging
>
> sickness
>
> death
>
> sorrow
>
> and loss

why seek the same again?

may 30

as a mother
protects her only child
with her life,

we too can cultivate
a boundless love
for all beings.

eventually our love
will pervade the whole world.

may 31

to reach others
       use soft but honest words
and have a kind
and sincere
       expression on your face.

june 1

a line drawn on water

vanishes in an instant.

our lives are like that line on the water.

life is short.

do not waste it.

june 2

want to change the world?

first,

change yourself.

june 3

when there are no thoughts
    of giving to others,
    of having offered,
    of sacrifices made,
we are advancing
towards awakening.

june 4

life is impermanent.
when others need help

do not hesitate
do not waste time
just help.

june 5

ego
self-importance
  keep us
    from forgiving others
    from forgiving ourselves;
pride
arrogance
  keep us
    from making peace with others
    from making peace with ourselves.

june 6

just as a rock
remains unmoved by the storm,
those who are wise
are unmoved by jealousy and pride.

june 7

everything that comes into existence,
living and non-living,
is connected to everything else.

nothing exists solely on its own.

june 8

all beings fear death.
all beings tremble at violence.
all beings yearn for safety and comfort.

put yourself in the place of another

can you then
threaten any being or
harm any being?

june 9

only when we are at peace

with ourselves,

will we be able to live

peacefully

with others.

june 10

all is impermanent:

    whatever arises will cease,

    all possessions will be lost,

    all meetings will end in separation,

    all life will end in death.

june 11

problems
do not cause suffering.

the cause
is how we choose to react
to the problems.

june 12

what matters is that we act with

sincerity,

respect,

honesty.

doing so, others will treat us

likewise.

june 13

in the service of others,
one places another's wishes and welfare
before one's own comfort
and personal preferences.
ideally, there is
no thought of like or dislike,
no feelings of superiority or pride,
no thought of self-benefit.
only the wish to help others.

june 14

into each life
we bring nothing
from each life
we take nothing

life after life
we come
we go

letting go will end the bringing and taking.
letting go will end the coming and going.

june 15

one who is free
from desire and sorrow
leaves all fetters behind
to pass beyond birth and death.
like a swan rising from a lake,
he moves on in peace
never looking back.

june 16

four things are constant:
no world lasts forever
        but will be swept away;
it is no shelter
        and protects not;
one will leave everything behind
        in passing to the next life;
life is incomplete
        and unsatisfying.

june 17

without barriers between people

our hearts can be filled with love.

such love can pervade

all of space

all of time.

june 18

anger

our own most terrible enemy

our greatest threat to peace.

june 19

all people wish to end pain

and find happiness.

the rest is secondary.

june 20

counteract greed with contentment.
if something new

comes our way

be content

if it passes us by

be content.

june 21

ideally we help others.

if we cannot help

at least

we should not harm.

june 22

with giving, we eliminate greed

with morality, we let go of afflictions

with patience, we dissolve hatred

with enthusiastic effort, we overcome laziness

with concentration, we calm pointless thoughts

with wisdom, we leave delusion behind.

june 23

wishing to hurt another,
        we experience anger
wishing to harm another,
        we experience animosity
when animosity festers,
        we experience hostility
when hostility is vented,
        it becomes cruelty.

june 24

to offer happiness,
we need to set aside
what we wish for
and provide others with
what they wish for.

with absolute sincerity

a few choice words

a simple act

a gentle smile

will ease apprehension

will dissolve sadness

and alleviate suffering.

june 26

in the midst of pain and sadness,

find love for all who suffer

the will to seek the truth

the heart to let go of the pain

the strength to find the way out.

june 27

the time may be short

but if we care enough

the time is enough.

june 28

we are not waves

crashing onto the shore

we are the ocean.

we are not individuals

alone and lost

we are the universe.

june 29

one who is

unaffected by things
    that elicit attachment,
unangered by things
    that produce irritation,
unworried by things
    that cause distress,

will leave unhappiness behind
    and dwell in peace.

june 30

loving others

is caring as much about

their happiness

as our own.

july 1

once the thought arises
    the word is spoken,
    and the deed is done.
        the thought
        the word
        the deed
will live on and impact others long after
    we have ceased
            thinking
                speaking
                    doing.

july 2

every thought we conceive
each act we commit
in the present,

creates the conditions
we will encounter
in our future.

july 3

in our last moments, we will ask:

what have i accomplished?
did i make a difference?

do not wait till then

ask now.

july 4

when about to speak
of one to another,
consider first if you would say it directly
to that person —
>   same intention
>   same words
>   same tone;
>   if not, it is best to remain silent.

july 5

sincerity in helping someone

is not accompanied

by the thought

"i am sincere"

nor followed by the thought

"i have done."

july 6

why become angry
when we fail to control others,
when we cannot control ourselves?

july 7

in the name of honor,

      men have acted ignobly.

in the name of peace,

      men have declared war.

july 8

most of the time,

we do not get what we desire.

some of the time,

this can be very fortunate.

july 9

awakening is the blossoming
of the mind and
of the spirit.

july 10

clinging narrows the heart;

giving broadens it.

clinging paralyzes the heart;

giving liberates it.

clinging darkens the heart;

giving brightens it.

july 11

it is far wiser to remain

honorable in silence

than to be

dishonorable in speech.

july 12

live contentedly with modest means
be   worthy instead of being praised
      think quietly
      talk gently
      act wisely
understand the past
care about the future.

july 13

the acorn and oak tree are separate

or are they?

the wood and flame are separate

or are they?

the act and actor are separate

or are they?

we are alone and separate from all else

or are we?

july 14

anger is a poison,

patience its antidote.

july 15

be wary of actions —
for the occasional reaction
can become an addictive habit.

july 16

the self is not an independent entity
with an individual existence,

but a convenient point of reference
which enables us to relate
to the world around us and
to circumstances we encounter.

july 17

why take pride in this body
and in possessions,
they do not last.

they are like castles in the sand
swept away by the tide;
like the scent of a flower
carried off by the wind.

july 18

a deeply rooted tree

which is cut down

will grow again.

like that tree

intolerance that is not uprooted

will rise again.

july 19

think first.
once a word is spoken
or an act committed,
we cannot undo the deed.
apologies
retractions
explanations
may lessen, but cannot undo
the harm done,
the pain that will remain.
think first.

july 20

with hearts pure and clean
like newly fallen snow,

with patience impartial and accepting
like the earth,

with compassion broad and all-encompassing
like the universe,

awakened ones help others.

july 21

when tempers are rising

and we do not know how to speak wisely,

it is best to remain quiet.

july 22

accord friends and

family

the same courtesy

we use for strangers.

july 23

when our caring for others
becomes immeasurable,
the mind embraces
the complete expanse of space,
and its capacity
encompasses the vastness
of the universe.

july 24

both body and mind
need to be healthy
to seek the way to enlightenment.

one's body needs to be
strong and healthy.

one's mind needs to be
peaceful and focused.

july 25

a lute's strings tightly strung will break

strings loosely strung will not play

with balance, comes a pleasing sound.

just as with a lute

serenity is found when one's life is

properly balanced.

july 26

greed
is wanting things
to occur as we wish.

anger
arises when we fail
to obtain what we want.

july 27

the love of those who are unawakened
arises from emotions.

the love of those who are awakened
is born of wisdom.
this love is
impartial,
unconditional,
all-encompassing.

july 28

our actions affect others,
just like a single drop of water
splashing on the ocean:
the resulting ripple
sets all the other
drops of water in the ocean
moving.

july 29

rivers join with the sea

which rises to merge with the clouds

falls to become one with the stream

and then rushes to return as rivers.

the cycle of life continues

interconnected

timelessly.

july 30

find some time

every day

to spend some time alone.

july 31

inflamed by greed,

incensed by anger,

confused by delusion,

obsessed by these,

overcome by these,

man causes his own suffering.

august 1

touch everything as if
you are touching a buddha.

for you are.

august 2

the wise have something to say.
but those who usually speak
are not necessarily wise.

august 3

there are three questions
we can ask ourselves every day:

have i been resolute
in helping others?

have i been trustworthy
when speaking with others?

have i been zealous
in practicing what i teach?

august 4

before starting a new undertaking,
look through the old
to see what can be used and
what needs to be discarded.

august 5

each new encounter is due
to a karmic link from a past life:
an affinity or an enmity
that can improve or worsen.
so, in each new encounter,
treat the other
with respect and consideration.

august 6

let go of expectations.

having done so
whenever something good happens
we will be content.
if things do not work out
we will not be disappointed.

either way
we will remain calm and balanced.

august 7

learn from the past but
  do not attach to it
  do not cling to it.
do not allow thoughts of it to overwhelm,
    like pains of old
    and sorrows past.

august 8

when looking, see clearly

when listening, hear keenly

when doubtful, pose questions

when working, be responsible

when speaking, be truthful.

august 9

one who is

sensitive to the needs of others

and

who perseveres in meeting those needs

will never be alone.

august 10

seek to benefit all beings
not just
those like ourselves.

august 11

if we taint pure water
with just a drop of poison,
all of the water will be tainted.

likewise

if we taint ourselves with thoughts
of duality—of *you*—of *me*
we will become tainted.

august 12

we are one

all part of one another.

if one part suffers and feels pain then

we also suffer and feel pain.

we are one.

august 13

kindness   without wisdom is folly.

valor   without wisdom is chaos.

august 14

since refusing to accept things as they are
does not make them go away,
would it not be wiser to learn
how to work with them?

august 15

when we make a mistake
and do not correct it,
we have truly made a mistake.

august 16

often we will have an impulse to give.
but then we start thinking
of all the reasons not to.
do not be deterred.
return to the initial thought and give.
each time we will return more quickly.
one day there will only be the first thought:

" give."

august 17

in gain, be honest
in giving, be thoughtful
in appearance, be warm
in demeanor, be respectful.

august 18

what i learned yesterday

was wonderful,

but what i learned today

was even more wonderful.

i had to release yesterday,

to learn today.

august 19

only question

how we treat others,

not how others treat us.

august 20

most of the time
we cannot control our circumstances,
but
every moment of time
we can control how we react
to these circumstances.

august 21

be like a buddha.
think like a buddha.
feel like a buddha.
pay attention
understand
work, walk
sit, smile.
be

like a buddha.

august 22

in teaching others

personify the teaching,

then others will wish to learn.

august 23

look within
...look deeper
...deeper still

everything we need is already here

within us.

august 24

existence is like a cloud.

from a distance it appears real.

but when we pass through it,

it is nothing.

august 25

if we cannot think solely of others for one day,
    do it for half a day.
if we cannot think solely of others for half a day,
    do it for two hours.
if not for two hours
    then one hour.
if not for one hour
    then one minute.

august 26

when there is resentment

anger will fester.

when resentment is no longer,

anger will likewise disappear.

august 27

just as the ice melts

　　under the springtime sun

disagreements and mistrust evaporate

　　amidst the warmth of kindness.

august 28

let all those you encounter

leave happier and better than they were before:

have gentleness in your eyes

loving-kindness in your smile.

august 29

even the largest jug

will become full

drop

by

d

r

o

p.

august 30

kindness will accomplish that

which force never will.

august 31

to offer happiness to others,
we need to know what they want,
and for this
we need to listen
and understand.

september 1

pursue wholeheartedly

that which is worthy,

put down completely

that which is not.

september 2

everything changes

everything disappears

nothing can be held on to.

september 3

nothing is

more virtuous than compassion

sweeter than serenity

purer than truth.

september 4

giving in to desire

we become prisoners

of our own greed.

renouncing desire

we are free.

september 5

it is not our friends

but our opponents

who give us the opportunity to grow.

september 6

the contented smile

at the end of the day

is born of helping others.

september 7

the teachings in the sutras

of

honesty

tolerance

impartiality

are not for others

but us.

september 8

although the body is   earthbound

         perhaps even   immovable,

the mind and spirit can

                through meditation

soar.

september 9

a momentary flash of anger

may seem inconsequential,

but it carries with it

the potential for a lifetime of suffering.

september 10

conflict in the name of religion

arises not because of a teacher's words

but due to humankind's

misunderstanding of those words.

september 11

the body in motion

the mind at peace

these are keys to

contentment and

happiness.

september 12

to overcome

strong negative feelings,

strengthen

those that are positive.

september 13

love often declines into hatred
but very rarely does
hatred grow into love.

september 14

a wise heart

   judges not

   craves not

   fears not.

it understands

and is no longer imprisoned by emotions.

september 15

nonviolence is not one option

it is the only reasonable option.

september 16

go through life

as if floating on water:

move with it

without drowning in it.

september 17

caring

begins with a simple question:

was my thought unkind?

september 18

there really is no choice:

exist in harmony

or

perish in dissension.

september 19

it takes more courage

to create peace,

than it takes

to create war.

september 20

generosity

morality

patience

diligence

concentration

wisdom

are the means—and the end.

september 21

anger from within

not from without

is the real destroyer.

september 22

if only we can realize that

the joy of others

is our own,

the pain of others

is our own,

we will then foster only joy

and never again cause pain.

september 23

one does not need to be arrogant

to think one can accomplish

something positive:

just optimistic.

september 24

changing the outside

will not fix the inside.

september 25

to truly help another

speak

truthfully and

honestly and

carefully.

september 26

disappointment
inevitably follows
expectation.

september 27

we are not isolated,

never alone.

what happens

on one side of the world

will inevitably effect the other.

september 28

anger begets anger
never peace
never love
never joy.

september 29

do not

emphasize the superficial differences—

instead,

celebrate the universal similarities.

september 30

our foolish ideas of what happiness is
keep us eternally searching
for the unfindable.

ensnared by these false thoughts,
we do not recognize the joy
that lies within us.

october 1

what matters is that we act

with sincerity, respect, and honesty.

doing so,

others will treat us likewise.

october 2

if you wish to see others smile...

...smile first.

october 3

we harm others

not because we are malicious

but

because we are careless.

october 4

ideally
we prevent unkind thoughts from arising,
but, initially, this is difficult to do.

until this can be accomplished,
strive to replace
unkind thoughts that arise
with those that are kind.

october 5

settle all disputes

before the end of the day

for there is no guarantee that

we will have tomorrow

to do so.

october 6

being close to one's teacher
is not living near the teacher.

rather it is
holding the teachings in one's heart
and sincerely endeavoring
to abide by them.

october 7

only speak words that are
necessary and
helpful.

october 8

the true friend is one who
            understands
            forgives
            forgets
our thoughtless words and acts,
offering us the kindness
of another chance.

october 9

let go of thoughts of "i"
    to benefit loved ones.
let go of benefiting loved ones
    to help those we know.
let go of helping those we know
    to serve all beings.

october 10

for good

or

for bad

everyone is someone

we can learn from.

october 11

who you are in this lifetime

is the result

of what you did in past lifetimes.

october 12

genuine happiness lies not

in getting what we want,

but rather

in not wanting.

october 13

where there is humankind

there is potential

for an act of goodness.

october 14

from craving

from arrogance

   come violence.

from trust

from honesty

   come peace.

october 15

one who thinks constantly
he deceived me
he hurt me
will never find
peace.

one who lets go of
resentment
hatred
will know
joy.

october 16

problems do not come
from outside of us,
but from within.

october 17

when there is no delusion

there is truth.

when there are no impure thoughts

there is sincerity.

october 18

focus not on what separates us

but on that which unites us.

october 19

as good thoughts increase just a bit
bad thoughts decrease just a bit.

as i created my future
so i can change it.

thought
by
thought.

october 20

there is no "i".

if there is no "i"
how can there be "mine"?

october 21

if today

i have not progressed

then today

i have already regressed.

october 22

the smallest good deed

that arises from a sincere heart

will spread throughout the universe.

october 23

when someone scolds me,
i become upset.

why is it that i am not upset when
this person scolds another?

october 24

one who is unselfish
can begin to care
for one who
is selfish.

but

one who is selfish
will care only
for himself.

october 25

a broad mind

doing a small deed

is considered great goodness.

a narrow mind

doing a big deed

is considered a small goodness.

october 26

always remember others' kindness

while

forgetting their weaknesses.

october 27

if someone hates me

but i still love them

then i have understood

and i have

achieved true results from my practice.

october 28

no lasting peace
can come from fear.

october 29

through giving   we are rich.

through grasping   poor.

october 30

until all people know peace,

we ourselves

will not know true peace.

october 31

by forgiving others
   for having hurt us,
we can
   let go of the painful past and
   create a happier future.

november 1

powerful people

        are concerned with winning,

while those with little,

              hope for kindness.

november 2

in separateness
lies the world's great suffering.

in unity
lies the world's true strength.

november 3

at times a person's actions irritate us
but not his words.
at times a person's words irritate us
but not his actions.
at times both words and actions
are irritating.

see the suffering behind these
ignore the irritation and
practice kindness.

november 4

ignorance leads to egoism,

egoism to selfishness,

selfishness to resentment,

resentment to anger,

anger to hatred,

hatred

to annihilation.

november 5

to find happiness
focus not
on what we want
rather
on what we have.

november 6

if we could only see

the suffering of others as our own,

mutual happiness would be possible.

november 7

we created our lives
we are responsible for them.

since

we are the ones
who created our lives,
we alone can change them.

november 8

if we can
   put aside our personal differences
      and understand that by nature
         we are all the same,
         we will be better able
         to treat all with respect.

in doing so,
   we will receive the respect of others.

november 9

everyone has a combination
of good and bad qualities.
the ones we dwell on
all too often
tell more about us
than about others.

november 10

we are the only ones

who can bring ourselves

peace.

november 11

an unkind thought
a careless word
can cause so much pain.

catch the thought.
hold the word.

november 12

even the smallest act

of kindness

is worthwhile.

november 13

the attainment of

contentment

simplicity

peace

far exceeds the attainment

of a vast fortune.

november 14

a gentle smile costs nothing

but

accomplishes much.

november 15

be patient.

be at peace.

november 16

thoughtfulness is
to care for others
even when we think
they may not deserve it,
for in reality,
we know very little.

november 17

pride is a dangerous trap.

if we think we understand everything—
we understand nothing.

november 18

persevere

    in determination

    in gentleness

    in humility.

let go

    of shortcomings

    of violence

    of pride.

november 19

imagine the pain of one who feels that

    no one cares

    no one understands

    no one will come to help.

november 20

when there is compassion

giving is not a burden

but a joy.

november 21

just as water can erode

the hardest stone —

sincerity can melt

the coldest heart.

november 22

what

is the price of patience

compared

to the cost of intolerance.

november 23

when the mind is quiet
with chattering thoughts at rest,

when the heart is gentle
with selfish thoughts given up,

the spirit will rise and soar.

november 24

there is a universal oneness
that pervades all existence:

just as

one cell in our body
        does not belong to another,
one being
        does not belong to another.

november 25

every day
make a fresh beginning.

november 26

the largest building begins
with one brick.

so too, we begin to improve
with one small act.

november 27

have hope for the future

but do not forget about today.

november 28

to be at peace

is

to create peace.

november 29

do not be concerned if the next person

is not doing his or her best.

instead, focus on how you yourself

are doing.

november 30

the young have ambition and energy
born of dreams,
the elderly wisdom and patience
born of experience.

tragically, those who are young forget that the elderly
also dream of happy children and caring families,
also work hard to improve their lives.

foolish youth will dismiss their efforts as outdated.

those more intelligent will
listen, learn, and grow wise.

december 1

believing in one religion
　　　　we should respect all religions.
being of one culture
　　　　we should respect all cultures.
living in one country
　　　　we should respect all countries.

december 2

buddhas   view all beings   as buddhas

bodhisattvas   as bodhisattvas

good people   as good

bad people   as bad

what am i

bad or good?

deluded or enlightened?

december 3

there is so much suffering already:
   unfulfilled expectations,
   personal confrontations,
   sickness, aging, and death.
why allow another's
skin color or spiritual beliefs
to be the cause of additional suffering?

december 4

viewing all equally
enlightened beings regard all beings
with impartial respect.

december 5

patience enables us
to counter anger
to interact harmoniously,
to recognize and overcome our shortcomings,
to react wisely in the face of adversity,
to stop blaming others for our problems,
to stay with a difficult undertaking without complaint,
disappointment,
resentment.
to find success and contentment.

december 6

when anger arises too quickly

to stop it,

try not to react rashly;

calm down,

find a way to diffuse it.

december 7

if we view others as

"strange"

or as a

"stranger"

we will lose the opportunity

to discover all that we hold in common.

december 8

just as

earthquakes bury

floods sweep away

and winds demolish

　　all of our physical accomplishments,

the fierce fire of anger consumes

　　all of our goodness and serenity.

december 9

nothing remains with us forever:

possessions are lost

or become unimportant,

people leave us

or we leave them,

places are left behind,

ideas change,

we move on.

december 10

why do we so easily become angry?

we do so because we are attached

to our view of who we are

to self-importance

to the concept of "i."

when the concept of "i" is threatened,

"i" very often strikes out in fear

in anger.

december 11

none of us are untouched by ignorance.
none of us are free from pain and grief.
none of us are safe from blind hatred.

none of us.

december 12

loyalty
is not to be applied blindly but judiciously,
as it is given to those who are
honest
ethical
and sincere.

wisely applied,
loyalty ennobles
both the giver and the receiver.

december 13

if we can rise above
our suspicions and defensiveness,
we will be able to share the similarities
and celebrate our diversity.

in this way,
all of us will benefit.

december 14

until young children are taught to do so,

they will not think of disliking another child

because his or her skin is another color.

it takes those who are older

to teach discrimination and hatred to a child.

it takes an impure mind

to sully an innocent one.

december 15

do not wait till you find
the perfect place to
be calm and content.
where you are
is already perfect.

december 16

in genuine giving

the magnitude of the act

does not matter.

the gratitude from the receiver

is inconsequential.

the sincere act of caring

is what matters.

december 17

love which comes from wisdom
is unconditional and nonjudgmental.
such love accepts another
as he or she is
and wishes only
for that persons' happiness.
such love brings happiness
to the one who loves as well.

december 18

by working together,
we come to realize
that no barriers
to religion, race or gender exist.

december 19

seeing the pain in someone's eyes,
or hearing the sadness
or worry in his or her voice,

how can we not care?

how can we not be kind?

december 20

each of us can do our best

to be as kind

as our heart allows.

december 21

in a task,

we can control the effort

but not the outcome.

focusing on the effort

will leave us contented

focusing on the outcome

will leave us frustrated.

december 22

joyfulness
is freeing others from unhappiness and
being sincerely happy for them
when they accomplish it.

it is a mental state
of great contentment and ease,
not to be misunderstood with happiness,
which is just a physical state
of feeling good.

december 23

we can choose

to lose ourselves
in anger and jealousy

or

to find ourselves
in patience and gratitude.

december 24

peace is more
than the mere absence of war.

it is the pro-active care
for the rights of others.

december 25

the serene and stable mind has
   no thoughts of preference
   no thoughts of reputation
   no thoughts of pride.
it no longer moves erratically
between feelings of great happiness
      and those of discomfort or sadness.
it is contented and
at ease with everything it encounters.

december 26

touch the beauty
and truth
within

to

reveal
and liberate
our natural joy.

december 27

an excellent way to counter selfishness
is through the practice of giving,
which invariably
puts the needs and wishes of others
before our own.

initially,
we may well feel that we are making a sacrifice,
but gradually
as we let go of our selfishness,
our giving will become spontaneous and joyful.

december 28

time has no beginning;
it has no end.

throughout immeasurable eons,
violence and conflict have abounded,
and body and spirit have been deeply wounded.
may the time for healing begin now.

december 29

immersed in anger,
polluted by selfishness.

as though ensnared,
humanity has been beset by ignorance.
but wisdom and compassion lie buried within.
may serenity and insight arise now.

december 30

we are not separate:
we are one.

seeming differences are inconsequential
for our hearts are the same.
respect and harmony are waiting to
awaken.

may universal peace begin now.

december 31

Dedication

May the goodness

accrued from this work

help to alleviate

the suffering of all beings

and enable them to find lasting happiness.

Ways to Reach Us

www.amitabha-gallery.org

www.chinkung.org

Australia [61]

Amitabha Buddhist Association of NSW

T: 2-9643-7588   F: 2-9643-7599

Amitabha Buddhist Association of Perth

T: 8-9306-8120   F: 8-9306-8366

Amitabha Buddhist Association of QLD

T: 7-3273-1693   F: 7-3272-0677   E: amtb@amtb-qld.org.au

Amitabha Buddhist Retreat Centre

T: 7-4171-0421   F: 7-4171-0413   www.abrc.org.au

Pure Land Learning Center of the NT

T: 8-8927-4988   F: 8-8947-3736   E: josephine@tchia.com

Pure Land Learning Center of Victoria
T: 3-9891-7093 F: 9891-7093 E: purelandvic@yahoo.com

Pure Land Learning College (Toowoomba)
T: 7-4637-8765 F: 7-4637-8764 www.amtb-aus.org

Canada [1]

Amitabha Buddhist Association of Ottawa
T: 613-723-9683 F: 613-723-6316 www.amtb-ottawa.ca

Amitabha (Six Harmony) Buddhist Organization
T: 416-265-9838 F: 905-947-1870 E: amtb6hcan@yahoo.ca

Amitabha Buddhist Society of Montreal
T: 514-257-1770 F: 514-525-6846 E: amtbmtl@hotpop.com

Amitabha Buddhist Society of Toronto
T: 416-293-0024 F: 416-292-6061

Infinite Light Amitabha Organization of Canada
T: 416-893-3366/265-9838 F: 905-947-1870 E: infamtb@yahoo.cz

United Kingdom [44]
Buddhist Education Foundation (UK)

T: 171-586-6923 F: 171-794-8594 www.buddhisteducation.co.uk

Hong Kong [852]
Hong Kong Buddhist Education Foundation
T: 2314-7099 F: 2314-1929 E: amtbhk1@budaedu.org.hk

Malaysia [60]
Amitabha Buddhist Society (Malaysia)
T: 03-4041-4101 F: 03-4041-2172 www.amtb-m.org.my/emid.shtml

Singapore [65]
Amitabha Buddhist Society (S)
T: 6744-7444 F: 6744-4774 E: abss@amtb.org.sg

Singapore Buddhist Lodge
T: 6737-2630   F: 6737-0877   E: sbl@sbl.org.sg

Taiwan [886]
The Corporation Republic of Hwa Dzan Society
T: 02-2754.7178   F: 02-2754-7262   www.amtb.org.tw

Thailand (662)
Amitabha Buddhist Society
T: 662-719-5206   F: 662-719-4356

United States of America [1]
Amida Society
T: 626-286-5700   F: 626-286-7988   E: amida@amtb-la.org

Amita Buddhism Society-Boston
T/F: 508-580-4349   E: amtb_boston@yahoo.com

Amitabha Buddhist Association of State Washington
T: 425-251-6822   F: 425-656-9789

Amitabha Buddhist Library in Chicago
T: 630-416-9422   F: 630-416-6175   www.amitabhalibrary.org

Amitabha Buddhist Library of Washington D.C.
T: 202-257-9533   F: 301-927-9596   E: amtbmd@hotmail.com

Amitabha Buddhist Society of Hawaii
T/F: 808-523-8909

Amitabha Buddhist Society of Houston
T: 713-339-1864   F: 713-339-2242

Amitabha Buddhist Society of Michigan
T: 734-995-5132   F: 734-995-5132

Amitabha Buddhist Society of New Jersey, Inc.
T: 856-751-7966 F: 856-751-2269 E: njbuddha@comcast.net

Amitabha Buddhist Society of NY, Inc.
T: 718-961-7299 F: 718-961-8039 E: amitabha_ny@yahoo.com.tw

Amitabha Buddhist Society of Philadelphia
T: 856-424-2516 F: 856-489-8528 E: amtbphila@hotmail.com

Amitabha Buddhist Society of Seattle
T: 206-624-9378

Amitabha Buddhist Society at UK
www.ku.edu/~amtb

Amitabha Buddhist Society of USA
T: 408-736-3386 F: 408-736-3389 www.amtb-usa.org

Amitabha Educational Center (Hawaii)
T: 808-262-5279   F: 808-262-4989

Amitabha Society of Las Vegas
T: 707-252-3042   F: 707-871-3542

Atlanta Amitabha Buddhist Society
T: 770-923-8955   F: 770-925-0618   E: mietoville@bellsouth.net

Dallas Buddhist Association
T: 972-234-4401   F: 972-234-8342   www.amtb-dba.org